ee Careful

od

B

et

Be

d

W9-BPP-192

appy

Good

Bee Careful

**MaKenzie**

A gift for

**Larry, patt & girls**

From

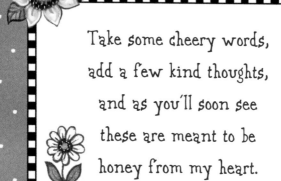

Take some cheery words,
add a few kind thoughts,
and as you'll soon see
these are meant to be
honey from my heart.

# Honey from My Heart
## for You

Illustrated by Debra Jordan Bryan

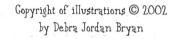

You're the kind of person
I'm so glad to know,
someone who
fills life's little corners
with a sunny glow.

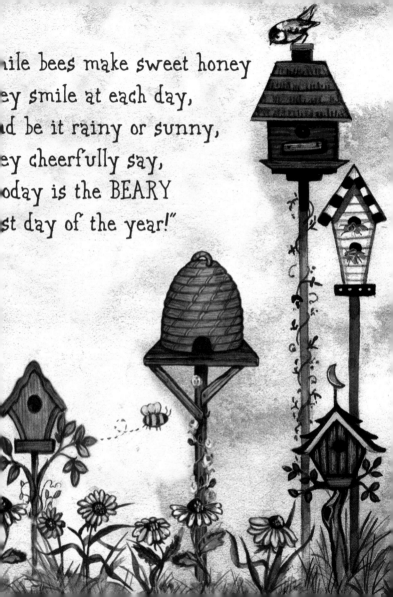

ile bees make sweet honey
ey smile at each day,
d be it rainy or sunny,
ey cheerfully say,
oday is the BEARY
st day of the year!"

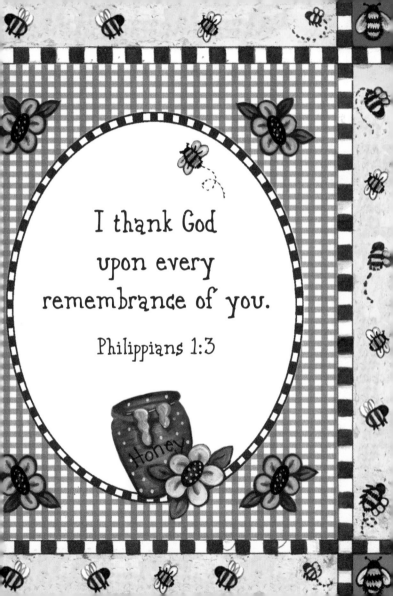

I thank God
upon every
remembrance of you.

Philippians 1:3

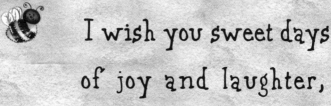

I wish you sweet days
of joy and laughter,
I wish you happy days
and smiles ever after.

# Some other things I wish for you:

_____

_____

_____

_____

The bees make
golden honey,
and you make
life sunny!

Can you count the honey bees,
in the sky so blue?
Nor can you count the ways
our Heavenly Father
cares for you.

Happiness is
like honey, . . .

it's more fun
when shared.

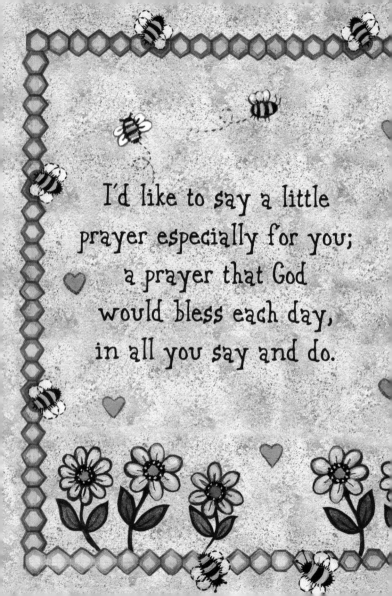

I'd like to say a little
prayer especially for you;
a prayer that God
would bless each day,
in all you say and do.

A little prayer for you:

_____

_____

_____

_____

_____

_____

Someone to share

someone to care,

someone to say,

"You'll be okay,"

... that is honey
for the heart!

I hope that you've enjoyed
this honey from my heart—
a short but
sincere way to say, . . .

Bee Sweet  Bee Kind

 Bee Happy

Bee Kind  Bee Careful

 Bee Good  B

Bee Careful Beehave

 Bee Sweet